Shattered to Mosaic

By Cynthia Kaitfors-Smith

Shattered to Mosaic

All the While Trusting God and walking with Jesus.

XULON ELITE

Xulon Press Elite
555 Winderley Pl, Suite 225
Maitland, FL 32751
407.339.4217
www.xulonpress.com

Paperback ISBN-13: 979-8-86850-099-2
Ebook ISBN-13: 979-8-86850-100-5

Thank You

To my amazing and loving husband, Michael,
who always believes in me.

To my remarkable sons, Jeremy and Joshua,
who are proud that I continue to grow in faith.

To our God who never leaves me.

Table of Contents

Acknowledgements

Zigzagging my way through betrayal and heartbreak would not have been possible without the love and support of my sons, Jeremy and Joshua Kaitfors, my brother, Tom, and his wife, Bev Collins (with endless phone calls), as well as my brothers, Cary and Dave Collins, with their loving check-ins.

I want to give special thanks to my aunt, Joyce Bohrer Blayney, for her prayers and support, to my cousin, Cory Jeanne Houck Cox, for her phone calls, cards, and texts, and to my step-grandmother, Loretta Ukulele, for her cards, phone calls, and gifts of love.

God opened doors to amazing church family friends. Thank you to Nancy and Richard Wayne, Paula and Bruce Muradian, and Pauline and Tom Jones for the countless dinners, prayers, fun, and fellowship with cards and game nights.

I was also blessed with loving and kind Christian colleagues. Mary Maddox, Janice Van Groningen, and Lupe Alcoser who were praying and supporting me all through those tough days at work when I lacked focus and confidence. I am blessed and thank God for bringing these amazing and caring ladies into my life.

There were many more friends (too many to mention) who reached out and popped up at just the right time. God made sure I was not only going to survive my divorce, but become the strong Christian woman He planned for me to be. To all who are in my life or who came and went in and out of my life, I thank you from the bottom and top of my heart.

Introduction

I grew up with a gift to gab, a wonderful imagination, and a creative spirit. I daydreamed my way through the school day, walked around the neighborhood with a girlfriend singing Christian songs, and took dance lessons from the time I was four.

I lived a simple life. Money was tight, we only had one car, and Mom stayed home to raise my brothers and me, but I must tell you that I felt like a millionaire when I walked into the public library and walked home with my arms full of books.

My imagination ran wild as I read. All of the people, the places, the plots - I loved every sentence, conflict, and times of joy. The places around the world I read about inspired me to learn about people, their goals, and their successes. I had a hard time putting a book down until it was finished. I can't even count how many nights my mother would scold me and tell me to turn out the lights and go to sleep. I swear she could hear the pages turning during the night.

So, with the love and joy of reading, it made sense to go to the bookstore for help when realizing I was about to learn my marriage was going to end. Unfortunately, the books I bought did not support, encourage, or strengthen my faith nor help me deal with my upcoming anguish.

As we go through life, there are going to be challenges, joys, and heartbreak. We cannot get away from it, yet how we travel through our trials, tribulations, and triumphs will give each of us a small sample of what is to come.

I have enjoyed life with all of the above circumstances, and I believe that I have come through it will a grateful heart, gratitude, and love for our God and Jesus Christ. I have known since I was a young girl that there is a God and Jesus Christ is our Savior who died on the cross for us.

However, as I was growing up, I lacked a personal relationship with Jesus and truly did not realize it was even important. I went to church, prayed, and worked on many different jobs within the church. I believed I was a good Christian and doing all of the right things. Looking back, I would now call myself a lukewarm Christian.

I prided myself and, honestly, probably bragged that I was doing all that needed to be done. I role modeled to my sons that going to church and praying at meals or bedtime was what we needed to do. I couldn't have been more wrong and learned this in the most difficult way.

Chapter 1

The Storm

January 2001

The day began as all other days: a little sunshine and clouds. I was loving the sweater weather and counting my blessings.

Until I found it...

A cell phone bill that had been hidden from me in the amount of over $800. I was filled with dread, first hoping we could afford to pay it and then questioning why most of the calls were to one number in Florida. I prayed it was not what I feared it was.

It was not just a rainstorm erupting; it was golf-ball-sized hail with torrential winds that ripped through me as I realized the phone number was *not* work related.

What do you do when all you have ever known has been taken away? Who can you turn to? The answer is simple: God and Jesus Christ.

Finding my way through heartbreak, shattered dreams, and a lost future was one of the most difficult challenges I had ever faced.

Years ago, my life took a harsh and demoralizing change. One chilly night in January 2001, my then husband admitted to having an affair, then instantly added he did not love me and wanted a divorce. To my best recollection, the conversation went just that fast and just that harsh.

Boom! In one instant, the life I had known for over thirty years was over.

For some marriages, there are loud, angry arguments, little quality time, or addictions that plague a relationship. For me, it was quiet and peaceful while I was visibly active in church and my husband's loving attention that surrounded my life for thirty years. Moreover, up to this point, I believed I was part of the 50 percent that would stay married to one man for the duration of my life. It is important to state that my marriage was not without disappointments or hurt feelings at times, but I presumed we had one of the "good marriages."

I was raised with the ideals that you share your thoughts and concerns, learn to listen to each other the best you can (we all have an agenda), and be kind and loving. When raising our children, many of my hopes and dreams were put on the back burner; however, I didn't regret any of our decisions as God always has a plan if we are walking in His path.

As a person who loves to visit, hash over the day, and make plans for the future, I was caught completely unaware of a brooding storm that would change my life. I think back to my naive and trusting nature and wonder if I could have forecasted the explosion that was about to erupt. Even now, I do not think so.

The question, "How do I get through the ordeal?" was not so easy. I began to hemorrhage emotionally. I felt incomplete. Half of me was missing. I had lost my identity! -Journal Entry (2001)

Many years later, I was asked if there were any red flags when we were dating, any idiosyncrasies that stuck out. I laughed and said no, but later, I thought about how my ex-husband stated he would date more than one girl at a time when he was young.

In my arrogance, I never believed he would dishonor his marriage vows. After all, our first date was to church and marriage was totally different than dating. And yet, if you don't honor the person you are with at the time, then why would you honor your marriage vows? So much for those red flags flapping in my face!

It is now many years since the beginning of my new life and I can look back with some perspective and clarity. Hindsight is 20/20, of course, and with that 20/20 vision, I should have seen it coming. However, I did not and because of my total trust to my then husband and our marriage vows, it knocked me to my knees. At the time, I didn't believe I could survive such a heart-wrenching experience.

I believed I had failed the Lord, my children, and myself. For whatever reason, I took all of the blame for the failed marriage. I had been left for another woman, so I must be the failure. - Journal Entry (April 2001)

Now, years later, I realized that wasn't correct. My ex-husband, Blake, made the choice to break his vows. He made the choice not to improve the marriage or talk about his thoughts, disappointments, and needs. He simply walked out emotionally and then later physically, leaving me distraught and shattered.

I have often wondered how others get through such an ordeal without faith in God and Jesus Christ, but then you hear or watch the news or read about horrific acts of revenge caused by infidelity. Sadly, if they had had God in their lives, an act of violence or vengeance would not be one of their options as to how to cope with their loss.

Aunt Joyce, my dad's sister, guided me through God's love and reminded me that vengeance was not mine to take, but left for God to handle. I am beyond thankful that I listened to her and had the Lord to lean on as I grew to become a strong Christian lady.

We live in a society where respect, kindness, and understanding are on the back burner. Our children are inundated with violent games, social media, and lack of Christian upbringing.

I always remind my Fresno Pacific University students that Christianity is one generation from extinction, and if we don't raise our children and grandchildren with the love of God and Jesus Christ, we have failed them, and Christianity becomes extinct. They are then left to learn from the secular society and social media.

So, you can see how easy it would be to ignore faith and constantly struggle with life challenges and disappointments. It is imperative to reach out to God and hang tightly to Jesus. Remember, God is only a prayer away. If you are trying to survive your upcoming divorce and your faith is not as strong as you would like, it is easy to talk with God.

If you do not know how to talk with God, just begin speaking as to a friend. He will listen and when you are finished speaking, be sure to thank God for listening. Then sit quietly or lie down and feel His love.

If you want or need more, say the Lord's Prayer:

> *Our Father in heaven, hallowed be your name, your kingdom come, your will be done, on earth as it is in heaven. Give us today our daily bread. And forgive us our trespasses, as*

> *we forgive those who trespassed against us. And lead us not into temptation, but deliver us from the evil. For thine is the kingdom, the power and the glory for ever and ever Amen.*
> Matthew 6:9-13

Then begin reading the Bible or Christian books that will strengthen your faith and trust in Jesus. The first book besides Bible scripture that brought me hope was *In the Eye of the Storm* by Max Lucado. This book made sense to me. It touched me with his many stories, his faith, and common sense about God's goodness and the miracle of Jesus.

I pray you can find a fulfilling book like the one that I read as you begin your recovery through divorce. It is a joy to know God continues to guide our footsteps through other Christian books, songs, and prayers. Remember to reach out, find what will fill your soul with love, and build your resilience.

When I began my journey through my divorce, it was like the blind leading the blind as the only knowledge of divorce was from a distance. I didn't have anyone immediately close to me who had needed my help or who would have shared their heartache and struggles.

All I knew was my faith, but I was so saddened, it was difficult to function with a clear mind. We need to make sure we are taking care of ourselves with focus and clarity; this is imperative if we are out in the workforce. A good example of this happened early on in my separation.

I was working in a fog, had a lack of focus, and was filled with anxiety. I was working as a school counselor and speaking with a parent regarding her son. He had been cutting himself and was having several behavioral and emotional struggles. The mother only spoke Spanish, so my interpreter asked the questions and then let me know what she was saying.

I began to ask a question regarding her son's father when I saw a strange look on the mother's face. I quickly asked my interpreter which mother I had in my office as I had two boys with the same names. One had a father at home and the other did not.

Oh, no! I realized I had the wrong mother with me. I began to crumble with tears running down my face. The mother also had tears as she didn't know why I was crying. I quickly began to pack up my belongings and tell the mother, "I am sorry, but I need to leave."

My interpreter was dumbfounded by my actions and explained to the mother that I was sorry, but had the wrong student. She explained further that I was not feeling well and needed to leave. I walked out of the building and drove an hour home, all the while tears rolling down my cheeks. I do remember receiving several phone calls from the school to check and make sure I was okay. Obviously, this was not my best moment, but it is a useful reminder to remember to please take time off if you need it. Self-care is vital to your overall health.

So, you can see why it is important to be clear-minded and functioning. I have always wondered what that poor mother must have been thinking. It was close to the end of the school year, so I never saw her again. I pray I did not traumatize her too much.

It is important to ask your spouse the difficult questions. I didn't as I was afraid to rock the boat. I knew some things were off, but chose to ignore the situation. If things are superficial or there is a lack of connection or respect, take the leap. First pray, then ask your spouse how they are feeling or what they need.

Many times, we fear the answer or do not want to upset the status quo; however, I would have gladly faced the tough questions rather than be blindsided by infidelity and an upcoming divorce. If I had been wise enough to trust in the Lord and have the tough conversations, who knows how it would have ended. Please remember, my marriage may still have ended in divorce, but I would not have been blindsided with his infidelity.

My prayer is that you address your marriage with grace, kindness, and understanding. It is easy to address the conversation with "you did this" or "you do not share your thoughts or feelings," but this will bring on negative and defensive conversation. Keep the Lord in every conversation by first praying for clarification and wisdom, then proceed with caution.

Since you are already facing the challenges and struggles of divorce, it is important to keep your hope of a wonderful future and life ahead of you. If you are thinking, "Well, that's easy for you to say," I am the poster girl for those Pollyanna thoughts. I have completely put myself in the hands of Jesus. It was a gradual walk that turned to knowing, but it is the choice we must make.

So, as we begin this walk toward the divorce and all of the trials and challenges that will arise, let us know full well that God has us and we will be successful.

Let's pray together. Dear Lord, as we put on the armor of God, our prayer is to speak with grace, mercy, and forgiveness. Allow our faith to be the center of our conversations as our love for You shines through us as we speak. Amen.

Chapter 2

Autopilot

I was out of sync. I cannot even express the lack of feelings, like being frozen, and the acute emotional pain as I had just lost my husband.

- Journal Entry (April 2001)

As I trudged through the beginning of my new life, I continued to be dazed and bewildered. I needed someone to put their arms around me and tell me I was going to be all right. I needed to know that I would be loved again and the hole in my heart with an anvil tied to it would not hurt or feel so empty. I longed to breathe again without effort and when I smiled, I would mean it.

I went into shock much later, realizing I had post-traumatic stress disorder (PTSD). I began functioning as a piece of equipment on autopilot. I walked around doing everyday chores. I went to work and spoke with colleagues, but felt numb. My parents were both dead; my mom had passed away a few months before and I was still grieving her loss.

My grown sons (ages thirty and twenty-seven at the time) had lives of their own, my co-workers lived in other towns, and before the separation, I had spent most of my time with family and had not cultivated friendships with other women. I had always spent weekends and holidays with family, but now, I felt so alone.

The word loneliness had taken on a whole new meaning as I had never experienced it to such a degree. Now, when I walked in the door, there was no one to greet me or ask how my day went. There was just silence and it felt like an empty tomb. In a single night, I had found myself isolated from anyone who might love me.

And yet God says, *Do not be anxious about anything, but in everything, by prayer and petition, with thanksgiving, present your requests to God* (Phil. 4:6).

As an educated woman with a degree in marriage family therapy, one would think all of this would be a walk in the park, but as the saying goes, "Only a fool heals thyself." I did ask myself one question though: what would I suggest to a client in this situation? One of the first things I always suggested was to journal their thoughts.

So began my written connection to God and Jesus.

Written Blessings

Why did I write this book? I want you to understand that God and Jesus are as close to you as you want them to be. Sing a joyful song, even if it is to yourself, that God loves you. If you lean on Jesus, trust in His ways, and stay close to Him in prayer, then you, too, will have the strength to walk through the toughest of challenges, the devasting hurts, and those feelings of being disposable and of little to no value.

Before we go any further, let's look at the things and feelings you will likely experience in the first few days and months of your separation and impending divorce:

- Shock, disbelief, denial, heartbreak, overwhelming sadness, anger, and jealousy
- Little sleep or appetite

- Hindered concentration
- Short term memory loss, weight gain/loss, and hair loss
- Loss of identity and control
- Debilitating loneliness that may lead to anger and fear
- A roller coaster of emotions, which may lead to anxiety and self-doubt

Please remember, though, that you always have strengths, even in the midst of devastating loss:

- Prayer life
- God's miracles along the way, which will be many
- Confidence in God's unfaltering care and provision
- Family and friends for support and encouragement
- Phone calls, emails, texts, gifts, and mail
- God-given talents and skills
- Journal, journal, journal
- And most importantly, take care of yourself

I also want to give special attention to humor. Don't forget to laugh. If nothing around you seems funny, go on YouTube and look up some good, clean comedy to get you laughing. It will bring a tiny smile to your face, and in that moment, you will feel better and start to see possibilities instead of only hurdles.

If you're like me and enjoy putting pen to paper or typing, jot down your strengths. Think about who you are and all of the resilience God has instilled in you. Then begin your journey.

____

____

____

____

____

So began my new life.

For I know the plans I have for you, declares the Lord, plans to proper you and not to harm you, plans to give you hope and a future. Jeremiah 29:11

I began journaling every night. Some nights, it would be one page or less; other nights, it would be page after page. Remember that, when writing to God, you are focusing on the correct message as He knows your hurts and disappointments, but also what lies ahead.

Surprisingly, a few months into my separation, as I was writing to God, I heard Him say to my heart, "*Cynthia, are you thankful for nothing?*" I kept journaling and again, I heard, *"Cynthia, are you thankful for nothing?"* Oh, my goodness! When God calls you by name, I pray you listen as it was such a wake-up call for me.

I realized at that moment that I had been continually grumbling to God about my hurts and losses and ignoring my countless blessings. After confessing to Him my unthankful heart and asking for forgiveness, I turned the page of my journal and began to ponder my blessings.

Is this where you are? Are you thinking only about your hurts, what you no longer have, or who you no longer have? If so, turn to a clean page in your journal and begin thanking God for all of His numerous blessings that are present in your life right now *and* the blessings that are to come.

Jot down a couple of blessings here:

____

____

____

____

As I began to think about all of the blessings the Lord had placed in my life, my focus began to shift toward happier thoughts. It was difficult at first, for sure, but as I thanked God for the family and friends who were taking care of me through phone calls, lunches out, cards, and emails, I began to see Him and His care for me instead of my feelings of abandonment and loss. I could see and feel that I was on the path to new joys, new provisions, and new life.

Though it still felt like it at times, I was not dying. My sons were healthy, strong, and supportive. My extended family lived thousands of miles away, but were still connecting through various acts of kindness. Slowly, but surely, I began to see my journey as an opportunity instead of just a painful slog. God had a mission for me, and as I began to heal, I began to see ways to bless others with my experiences of both loss and restoration. I was gaining new ways to help others and that made my truly painful situation feel potentially useful instead of just awful.

So, every day, I had a choice to focus on my loneliness or my blessings. But choices aren't made by accident. We must first choose to spend time with God, reading His Word, and praying to Him so that our hearts and minds can be directed toward Him and then, as He promises, "...all these things will be added unto you" (Matt. 6:33). Even through the tough days and nights, I continued to thank God for showering me with His love, grace, and mercy every day.

Let us then approach God's throne of grace with confidence, so that we may receive mercy and find grace to help us in our time of need. Hebrews 4:16

I began putting this scripture to the test by inviting friends to the movies or out to lunch so we could laugh, talk, and have a great time! This diminished my feelings of loneliness and helped me to see and feel God's blessings and love.

There was still at least one lingering problem: too often I had little emotional energy. Nearly every step I took felt like the final step of a one-hundred-mile walk, uphill, in the snow.

I pray that if your strength and energy level are not what you want them to be, you will lean on God like never before and trust Him for everything you need, even the strength to reach out to a friend.

Dear friend, remember to love and congratulate yourself for making the call and then thank God for the strength to reach out. Each time we allow ourselves to be with others, our stamina and energy levels increase, which helps us each minute of every day.

My townhouse had a balcony off the bedroom that became home for a couple of doves and their baby. One evening around nine, I heard a commotion outside. Much to my distress, I saw that the baby dove was hurt and lying on the ground. I could barely help myself, let alone a baby bird. So, I made some phone calls and found a woman who works with the national parks helping wounded birds.

She agreed to take my little bird, but only if I brought it to her. Once again, I was forced out of my comfort zone and called some church friends. My dear friends, Paula and Bruce, had taken me under their wings with all kinds of support, so there I was, making a late-night phone call to them, my mind as scared and helpless as that of the baby bird.

I told them the situation and how I was afraid to pick up the bird. These dear friends came to my house an hour later with a box and towel. Bruce picked up the baby bird and gently put it in the box so I could take it over to the wonderful woman who helps these little ones.

> *Therefore, I tell you, do not worry about your life, what you will eat or drink; or about your body, what you will wear. Is not life more than food, and the body more than clothes? Look at the birds of the air; they do not sow or reap or store away in barns, and yet your heavenly Father feeds them. Are you not much more valuable than they? Can any one of you by worrying add a single hour to your life?* (Matt. 6:25-34)

We are surrounded by loving, caring people who will go out of their way for others. Once you have been on the receiving end of this kind of sacrificial love, be sure to go out of your way for others. It's an extraordinary way to give back and show the love of God.

Ask and it shall be given to you; seek and you shall find; knock and the door shall be opened (Matt. 7:7).

Learning to Live Alone

Let's take a moment and think about the disciples. When Jesus returned after the resurrection, He found them in the upper room hiding. They were hiding! I can't even imagine how frightened they must have felt. Were they giving each other support and encouragement? Or were they, like me, feeling alone and consumed with "it's all about me"?

I didn't know how frightened I could feel until I realized I was going to spend the rest of my life "alone." When I think back on it, I'm not sure if I was frightened by the idea or just aware of the realization that, for the first time in my life, I had no one around me at home. I had lived with my parents, my college roommates, and then my husband and children.

I can remember Janice, a close co-worker, asking me if I feared being alone in my townhouse. Surprisingly, I answered that I was not alone since I always felt God's presence.

My son, Josh, was single and some of my family wanted him to return to Fresno to take care of his mother. I told Josh that it wasn't his job to take care of me and that I was doing just fine, so to speak. However, he ended up moving back to Fresno anyway to finish earning his teaching credential.

Though his company would surely be welcomed at times, my saving grace was being numb and on autopilot. Are you feeling an overwhelming numbness as you go through your separation or divorce? Do you think this is how the disciples felt when they were grieving? Perhaps. There were twelve of them and, as you know, there's comfort in numbers. Most of the time, I was making this challenging walk by myself. Are you feeling this loneliness, too?

How are you dealing with it? You can journal your thoughts and ideas below as it may give you solace and comfort in your sadness.

Knowing I had to make this walk with only God and Jesus made my sole focus to trust God in all ways and hold tightly to Jesus.

That was the beginning of my personal relationship with Jesus that continues strongly to this day.

I began appreciating the small things in my life, like sitting outside, listening to Christian music while writing to God, and enjoying the kinds of beautiful evenings found only in California.

As I look back on those nights, I can see that was I getting tiny glimpses of the joy that was developing ever so slowly. My hope is that you, too, will begin to have those tiny glimpses that only God and Jesus can provide.

This would be a great time to journal your own glimpses of God's joy.

____

____

____

____

____

There were days when I didn't think I could get out of bed for work and when I arrived home, I could not wait to pull the covers up over me and shut out the painful world. I cried. I prayed desperately for help. And then I cried again as if I had never cried before.

I remember sitting on my stairs many days after work, crying and asking God for strength, for answers, and for the pain to stop.

Even so, because of my faith in Jesus, all was not lost, even in my daily tears and fears. I had always known a strong relationship with Jesus, but I was learning just how strong He was in my painful walk-through separation and divorce. I also knew that whatever God allowed in my life would never be without His constant companionship and power.

I had also earned a master's degree in marriage family therapy, for heaven's sake. My knowledge and skills helped me survive and know what to do when my feelings threatened to overtake my mind: journal! Then journal some more and keep journaling whenever I began to feel overwhelmed.

I bought a journal and began to write in it just a couple of days after my husband admitted to having an affair and asked for the divorce. As I look back on those stormy days, which turned to years, thanks to PTSD, I see the miracles God placed before me: family support, lunches out, new girlfriends, and an inner strength that was growing by leaps and bounds. I didn't realize how much grace He could bestow on me or how He had my future planned for opportunities I hadn't even dreamed of. One of those opportunities came in my adjunct faculty position with a Christian university. What a blessing!

I remember sitting on the bed and listening to my husband say the words, "I don't hate you. I don't dislike you. I just don't love you." I sat there thinking,

Of course, you do not hate or dislike me, but what are *you saying?*

The unimaginable was happening and I had no control over it. Or did I?

I was trying to comprehend what he was saying, but my brain had no compartment for such shocking words, and I could feel the numbness course through my body. My survival mode was kicking in. I went into autopilot. It became difficult to breathe. Even though I begin to feel paralyzed with sadness and couldn't keep my thoughts straight, my heart knew that my relationship with Jesus was going to see me through.

To this day, I have wondered how people endure their trials and tribulations without God and Jesus Christ. Is this something you are struggling with?

What are the ways you can help yourself? Be sure to give yourself time to reflect, pray, and reach out for help when feeling lonely and overwhelmed.

Take My Hand

Wouldn't it have been great to read the journals of our disciples after the death of Jesus and know how they dealt with their grief and fears? Were they supporting each other? God gives all of His children unique gifts and skills, even the disciples, to help us adapt to and even overcome difficulties.

I have been blessed with resilience and strong faith, which have helped me walk through the tough times. Because my faith was strong, it made it tough to believe God would not want us to reconcile and keep our marriage intact. This belief kept my thoughts on the past and not on what was happening in the present.

It is important to remember that there are five stages of grief: denial, anger, bargaining, depression, and acceptance. No matter how strong my faith, I still had to walk through all of the stages and I was at the beginning with denial.

My denial about the upcoming divorce and my wish to fill the huge void in my heart felt so overwhelming that I had trouble taking deep breaths. I was not listening to God as I was struggling to get through each moment. Why was it so difficult? Why wasn't I getting any answers?

Be merciful to me O Lord, for I am in distress; my eyes grow weak with sorrow, my soul, and my body with grief. Psalm 31:9

How could someone hurt another person so deeply, not care, and then walk away without a backward glance? I still do not have the answer to that, but it has changed how I treat people, how I listen to what others are saying, and how to roll with the punches. I am so thankful for the mercy God showed me during those days.

One night, about four months into my loneliness, tears, and heartache, I could not stand my depression. It was 8:45 p.m. and all I wanted to do was go to sleep. So, I closed the drapes and asked God for sleep.

I fell asleep immediately and began to dream.

> *I was standing in front of very large bleachers. My brother, Tom, and his wife, Bev, were sitting at the top of the bleachers calling my name. "Cyn, come up here with us." I waved, smiled, and began to look around for the stairway. I could not find it and the bleachers were so crowded; my sister-in-law kept calling my name. "Cyn, come on." I began to*

feel uncomfortable; after all, I was standing in front of thousands of people. No one would help me as I paced back and forth; they all just stared at me. Suddenly, I heard my name being called, "Cynde, give Me your hand." I looked around and again, I heard, "Cynde, give Me your hand." I saw an outstretched arm belonging to an extremely handsome man with such love in His eyes. It was not so much a physical beauty, more like an inner love.

I reached out to Him, put my hand in His, and instantly felt a love unlike any I had ever felt before. It raced through my body for a glorious, exhilarating instant. Then I heard, "Now, you may go up." As I looked toward the bleachers, I saw that He (Jesus) had pointed to the bleachers where an opened stairway was waiting for me. It was a wide stairway, without any hinderance of people and not steep or difficult to ascend.

I awoke immediately and realized that I had just held onto the hand of Jesus. I also knew I had to continue to hold on to Him as I walked through the divorce. I knew it was going to be messy, uncomfortable, and that no one was going to physically hold my hand. I had to rely on Jesus and realize that only through Him could I accomplish the journey ahead of me. When I shared this experience with my pastor the next day, he told me I had had an epiphany.

Yes, I had held Jesus's hand. Wow! I still wonder why I was given such a blessing and privilege. After experiencing my incredible dream, I finally understood what "born again" really meant. I felt jubilant, over the top with joy, more alive, more in touch with God, and understood the love Jesus has for each of us. I wanted to share this with everyone. I wanted to talk to my family who had been supporting me each day, my new friends, and my colleagues.

For me, the sad part was that not all people were ready to hear what I wanted to share. Some of my family thought that I had gone off the deep end. To them, I was a Jesus-loving, Jesus-talking, good-news-spreading gal. I had an inner joy that I wanted others to experience as I bubbled over with His love and joy. And yes, I had to share it.

That was disappointing to say the least, but I understood their hesitancy since I may have acted the same way. Unless we have an epiphany or a simple experience of God's presence, we remain unbelievers.

Remember doubting Thomas? He needed to see and feel the nail holes in Jesus. Shame on our little faith. I think that is what makes us human, unfortunately, and it didn't stop me from spreading my good news.

Somehow, I knew that God wanted me to do more than just get through the divorce. He wanted me to help those who would come after me so they could also be encouraged to cling to Jesus and grow in their spiritual walks. Little by little, day by day, I began to fully realize that I was going to make it through my heartache; however, it was going to require constant faith, trust in God, and a continuous abiding in Jesus. I also knew that, even with Jesus's sustaining grace, it was not going to be quick, painless, or easy.

Sometimes, every moment of the day felt like a chore. I continued on autopilot much of the time and still felt flabbergasted when I had made it through another day, week, and month. I praised and thanked God for getting me to each small, yet new triumph.

I will never forget the day I realized I had made it one whole year. I was driving to work and talking with God when the milestone hit me. I praised Him at the amazing realization that not only had I survived a whole year, but I didn't feel defeated or despondent.

I was jubilant and filled with love for God who takes care of each of us every day. I was still numb, but it was a different kind of numb. I wasn't crying all the time. I was still achingly lonely and even in denial a bit, but I had made it a full year. I congratulated myself.

If you are wondering what I mean by denial, it's this: I truly believed that God would not allow our marriage to fall apart. I continued trusting in my wants and desires instead of trusting what God wanted for me. At times, I would set the table and put out a place setting for my ex-husband. I would say a blessing over the meal and then ask the Lord to bring my ex-husband home.

I would find reasons to see or call him. I wanted him to see me in my new life—thinner, sporting a younger hairstyle, and enjoying my independence. Of course, this was wasted energy as my denial blinded me to the facts. My ex-husband was not interested and couldn't care less about any of my changes.

Another example of my denial was my thinking that he would put me first before other women. At lunch one day with a girlfriend, who was also a therapist, we began talking about my upcoming divorce. She asked me if I thought I was number one in his life. I answered no, and she responded with, "Correct, and you never will be again." Ouch! At that moment, I realized I was never going to be a major part of my soon-to-be ex-husband's life.

Although my friend's comment was brutally honest, I needed to hear it. I was still clinging to my own expectations and agenda, so it was going to take more time to sink in. I still believed, deep in my heart, that God did not want our family to break apart, yet I couldn't force even God's ideal plan for each couple on someone else. Getting married takes two, but getting divorced doesn't, not anymore, at least.

I also needed to remember that God gives us freewill, and Blake was using his to remove himself from my life to joyfully skip, jump, and run to his new one.

What I needed most to do at that moment was look toward the future and prepare for the journey, whether it was my desire or God's best interest. By slowly letting go, I could begin to think about what God had next for me. I could even start to get just a little excited about what miracles God might have in store for me. I was beginning to feel an inner joy that would bubble up and fill me with exuberance, then anxiousness. By God's grace, I would remember to give myself healthy self-talk and put one metaphorical foot in front of the other. A new life was opening up for me.

Love never gives up, never loses faith, is always hopeful and endures through every circumstance. 1 Corinthians 13:7

If you are in the denial stage of your grief, what are you hanging onto? What are you doing to prolong the inevitable? Write your thoughts in your journal.

Chapter 3

Frozen and Disposable

At times today, I felt frozen, not able to do anything but sit. Why did he have to have an affair? It's like a hot knife to my heart. - Journal Entry (March 2002)

Were you blindsided by your divorce? Did you argue, fight, or disagree all the time? My husband and I had none of these, so I was truthfully astonished when I learned that my husband had been unhappy. Why didn't he ever tell me? Didn't he want a happy marriage? Doesn't everybody?

Being betrayed leaves one so empty, so insecure, and it destroys one's self-confidence. It left me feeling disposable, like old trash that was no longer useful. Nevertheless, I tried to save our marriage. Surely, we could fix things; after all, we had a lifetime of memories, a lifetime in front of the Lord, and God was not going to let me fail at such a righteous goal.

So, I went searching for answers. What did I do wrong? How could I have changed things? Will I get a second chance? I *needed* a second chance!

I hope that by now you're seeing a pattern in my thinking. All my thoughts revolve around "I." **I** wanted to control the situation and **I** wanted to fix it. When I began to pray, it was not for God's plan, but for my own.

Many months into my divorce, both of my sons stated at different times that, "Maybe God wants something different for you," and, "Maybe Dad is holding you back."

The comfort my sons were giving me did not fall on deaf ears, just stubborn ones. I still wanted to fix it. I wanted my family intact. I would ask God and Jesus for help and then proceed to tell them what was best for me. I have always thought God and Jesus must have a great sense of humor and enormous patience; otherwise, how could they deal with my arrogance? But I am getting ahead of myself.

When we are going through deep trials and tribulations, it's difficult for others to understand our sadness, fears, and broken hearts. The depth of betrayal is beyond words.

The Joys of Motherhood

One of the constants in my life was my sons. They gave such love in their own ways. In the beginning, my older son, Jeremy, called each day to get me to work. We would talk and share support as well as our mutual love. Bless his heart, he did this for two months. I also believe that since Jeremy was married with a little girl, our impending divorce was not as devastating for him as it was for his brother.

Joshua, my younger son, would stop by with take-out so we could eat together and talk; however, our early visits were stressful and awkward. We were both grieving and it felt like the blind leading the blind. Joshua had idolized his father and to know that he had cheated on me and wanted a divorce was deeply painful and disruptive.

Through it all, we three became stronger and closer to God. We found it easier to pray together, talk about the love of Jesus, and the importance of building a personal relationship with our Lord and Savior. We were no longer afraid to discuss our hearts, feelings, and disappointments. It is true that good things blossom, despite hurtful situations.

An example of our bonding, sharing, and laughing was in the beginning of the separation. I flew to Arizona to spend time with Jeremy and his family for a long weekend. While there, my two sons were in constant contact with each other. I thought it was about me, but I would soon find out. When I arrived back at home, Joshua picked me up.

He had a strange grin and I thought, *Oh, no. What else could be wrong?* So, I asked and he turned to the side so I could see his arm. I was unsure what to look for until he lifted the shirt sleeve. Let me stress that I detest tattoos and always discouraged my sons from getting them, but once I saw the tattoo on his arm, I began to laugh and said, "Aren't you glad I am going through a divorce? Otherwise, I would be a raving lunatic." We laughed and he stated that Jeremy was getting his at that moment.

I then asked, "What do the Japanese symbols stand for?"

He said, "Honor as we never want to be men without honor like our father." (It is important to note that their Grandmother, my mom was Japanese, therefore Japanese symbol).

Wow, what can a momma say when she hears that?! God is amazing and wonderful and allowed my sons their way to display their grief and disappointment. It was a way for me to breathe and understand life was going to be different and we needed to flex and begin anew.

One of our survival techniques was making new traditions. At our first Thanksgiving, Joshua and I drove to San Francisco for fish dinner. Even though we were sad, it was so much better to celebrate away from familiar surroundings that were full of old and heartbreaking memories. I can just picture us choking down a turkey dinner with all of the fixings without crying or overly focusing on sad thoughts.

Instead of a large, gorgeous Christmas tree during that holiday season, we displayed a small tabletop version with all new decorations. If you feel similarly motivated to change your surroundings during the holidays, give yourself permission to totally redecorate.

Another new tradition I began was buying a small bouquet of flowers from the grocery store twice a month. It lifted me up and I loved having some of God's beauty on my table. By the way, I still have flowers on my dining room table. I love carnations!

The Lord made me a strong woman who never lacked for an opinion or a short story, yet after the betrayal, I was brought to my knees. The feeling that you are no longer lovable, that you lack what it takes to be worthy, is one of the worst feelings a person can have. If this is where you are at right now, I understand your lack of emotions and low self-worth. Your inability to navigate the simple chores in your daily life is unbearable.

The feeling of being disposable, not being good enough, and being a failure ate at my very existence. I was no longer equipped to handle the simplest tasks. I was just fortunate to *breathe moment to moment*. I finally understood the meaning of that statement.

I wasn't sleeping or eating. I had lost a great deal of weight and hair! Stress can be *wonderful* that way, but for me, the weight loss was a weird sort of blessing in the midst of great sorrow. I would even joke about my new weight loss program. "It may not be for everyone, but it sure worked for me!" Using humor helped me tremendously when my very existence was just a body desperately clinging to life, *any* life, no matter how shallow. My mantra was simple and unrelenting, "Mend my marriage."

But, my friends, my marriage had ended many months before Blake ever asked for the divorce, I just didn't know it. Unfortunately, denial can be a stubborn enemy and I was determined to reattach what had been clearly severed. My survival depended on it, at least I thought it did.

I don't believe I had ever felt such sorrow, even when my parents died. Yes, losing them was a deep hurt, but my heart accepted its inevitability and I took the grieving process as a natural journey instead of one to deny at all costs. The hole in my heart over losing Blake was deeper than any idea I had ever encountered or conceived. My thoughts were uncomplicated and straightforward: how do I get through today, tomorrow, and beyond?

From the first days, I knew my only hope was in the Lord. I prayed and clung to all of the scripture I had heard throughout my life. If you didn't grow up reading the Bible or memorizing scripture, start now. If you read your Bible, but not very often, do it more. Do it every day. You may be busy, but you should never be too busy to spend time with our Savior and

Lord. Your very life may depend on it. It will help you heal, it will help any children you have to heal, and it will help you begin to live the new life God has for you, even if that life feels like it has been born of sinful decisions.

We've covered a lot of territory. Take time to write down any thoughts you are now having and ask God to direct them toward His perfect will.

____

____

____

____

____

Overcoming Denial

Through it all, I continued expecting my husband to come to his senses and come back to me. Afterall, I trusted God and He knows what's happening. He hates divorce, so it's only a matter of time before things work themselves out. Denial! Denial! Denial!

By denial, I mean the thought that Blake would realize that he had made a huge mistake and, with

God's help, would come home—the home we had shared for so many years.

Have I not commanded you? Be strong and courageous ... The Lord your God will be with you wherever you go. Joshua 1:9

What I did not know was that my husband's affair had been active for over a year. When he broke the news, he claimed to have been with her only one time, which in my mind meant there was hope for reconciliation.

As I frantically sought solutions to rebuild our marriage from the shattered pieces it had become, I tried suggesting counseling to my husband. After all, we had never discussed being unhappy or unfulfilled, but rejoiced at the blessings of an amazing family and life. Most importantly, he had been unfaithful only "one" time.

Oh, how far from the truth could I have been! Again, I heard a harsh tone as he flatly refused to even discuss counseling. He "needed to be happy!" He didn't want to live the rest of his life like "this!"

Like "what," exactly? What does that even mean?

My brain swirled in disbelief as I wondered if the man sitting near me was even the same man I had been married to for so many years. What was he?! Where did my happy-go-lucky guy go? The guy who spent time with his family and participated in church services? I was utterly bewildered.

The confident woman I was the day before was gone and I had no idea who the woman before the mirror was. I felt like I had lost my whole identity. I was broken, weak, and suddenly felt much older. Being left for another woman, and a younger one at that, leaves one feeling vulnerable and quite unsure of her value.

How does one work their way through the challenges, enormous devastation, and horrible feelings of disposability? I was unsure if I could breathe the next moment; however, I knew the only way through this nightmare was to trust and lean on God.

In Thee, O Lord, do I put my trust. Psalm 71:1a (KJV)

If this is where you are, please know that God's plan for you is far better than you could imagine or dream. His plans are perfect and we are blessed with His mercy, grace, and forgiveness. Trust Him and let your life follow His path. It will take discipline and time, but the outcome is far beyond any human expectations.

Chapter 4

Building My Trust

Trusting God was easy, but how do I stop the emotional hemorrhaging? Or the feeling that I lost half of myself? I was incomplete. I never knew the hurt could penetrate so deeply or be so debilitating.

- Journal Entry (April 2001)

How do I go on from here? I was so disconnected and lost. It felt like an anvil had been tied to my heart. I clearly understood the expression, "I am not sure I can breathe the next moment, the next hour." I had no ability to focus. I couldn't even watch any television program as I had lost interest in all shows or movies.

The only thing I could concentrate on and find the energy to pursue was journaling my thoughts. I felt an urgent motivation to get them on paper, so I could be sure that I wasn't losing my ever-living mind.

The day after my husband asked for the divorce, I bought my first journal. I poured out my thoughts and pain onto the pages, all the while promising to cling tightly to God.

Is it time to start a journal of your own? What do you want to share with God?

If you're finding it was difficult to think beyond the failure of your marriage, it was difficult for me, too. In fact, I was feeling the weight of several failures:

- The failure of my marriage
- The loss of my identity as a wife and life partner
- The feeling that I had failed not only my husband, but my children and God, too
- My failure as a wife. Maybe if I had been "perfect," he wouldn't have left me for someone else. Then I wondered, "What *makes* the perfect wife?"
- Constantly clean house, clothes all washed and put away, four-course candlelit meals, and, of course, a sexy lady waiting on her husband, never tired or out of sorts

What traits do you think make up the "perfect wife"? Does the perfect wife even exist? Should we even try?

Write them down in your journal. Doing so might make you feel better as it will help you see how unattainable (and humanly unreasonable) perfection really is.

It's important to remember that if our spouse has decided to leave, even that perfect wife wouldn't change his mind.

At the time, it seemed clear to me that I was the problem. After all, my husband was delighted and ecstatic with his new beginning. He walked away with bliss in his heart. I, on the other hand, had to pick up the pieces of a failed marriage. I was humiliated and embarrassed. He left me for someone "better," or so I thought.

Now, I must mention that, while feeling all of the anguish as deep as it was, I also knew in my heart that God was still there. He was telling me to reach out to others and to join a women's Bible study. I could hear the increasingly loud message from the Holy Spirit pulling me toward Him, compelling me to listen and obey.

Four weeks into our separation, I finally surrendered my will to His and ventured beyond my comfort zone.

I went to my first women's Bible study, scared, nervous, and disheartened, but always following my faith.

The Lord is my Rock. My fortress and my deliverer. My God is my rock, in whom I take refuge. Psalm 18:2a

As I walked into that Bible study, I was about to experience my first miracle. I didn't know it at the time, but this was the beginning of my personal relationship with Jesus Christ.

We were about to study a women's devotional by Beth Moore. The first question was, "Do you believe in God?" I quietly answered, "Of course." As the other women were talking, I was thinking, *What a silly question*.

Then the second question, "Do you trust God?" This question hit home like no other. Maybe it was because I needed answers or maybe because God's timing is perfect. Or *maybe* it was the first time I had ever heard the answer from inside my soul.

Yes, I trusted Him; however, that didn't make the healing process any easier. What it *did* do was help me to prioritize the most important things in my life.

Through my journaling, I was in constant contact with God and our Savior, Jesus Christ.

I accomplished this contact through prayers, conversations, and writing. Even my music was tuned to the Christian stations and the only television I watched at that time was faith-based. I needed to saturate my soul with God's love and Jesus's compassion.

I was learning to trust Him in all ways. As I listened to the ladies in our Bible study, I heard many different answers to the question, "Do you trust God?" Each woman was in a distinct place with God and her relationship with Jesus. My walk with Jesus was in its infancy.

I can remember journaling and wondering, "Who do I talk to? God, Jesus, or the Holy Spirit?" I was embarrassed to not know. It seemed impossible after having attended church all of my life; however, my godly life had been only superficial, unbeknownst to me at the time.

It was at that moment that I knew I must believe in and trust God and that He will help me make the walk through this hell. It must be hell; otherwise, I wouldn't feel so paralyzed and helpless.

Trusting God

We must understand that no one can fully carry us through our difficult walks except Jesus. Therefore, four weeks into my journey, I committed my life to Him. This was the beginning of my personal relationship with the Lord.

I decided to trust the Lord no matter how devasted I became or how sad, lonely, or broken I felt.

I had decided to continue my financial support for my younger son, who at the time was finishing his credentials. When I realized that it would take me years to pay off the loan, I had friends tell me to file for bankruptcy. But it was my bill and my choice to go into debt; therefore, the Lord and I would pay it back together.

It took several years (ten, to be exact), but when I finally paid it off, I thanked God for constantly keeping me solvent while making each and every payment.

I trust in your unfailing love. I will rejoice because you have rescued me. Psalm 13:5

Jesus Praying

It made me wonder if this was how Jesus felt when praying in the garden of Gethsemane—sad, broken, and alone.

"Father, if you are willing, take this cup from me; yet not my will, but yours be done." And being in anguish, he prayed more earnestly, and his sweat was like drops of blood falling to the ground. Luke 22:42, 44

Jesus asked His disciples to join Him in His night of prayer, but they all feel asleep. Exhausted from sorrow, Jesus asked, *"Why are you sleeping? Get up and pray so that you will not fall into temptation."* Luke 22:46

In our painful passages, we have the comfort of knowing that Jesus will not fall asleep. He'll be there for us, always, and we can be strong while standing arm-in-arm with Him, lest temptation lead us astray.

As I learned and grew in my personal relationship with Jesus, my heart and soul were opened to His great love, mercy, and grace. I received so many "love touches" from God. They came in the form of encouraging thoughts from the Lord like, "You will get through this," and through special phone calls or dreams that suggested all would be well. At times, I would dream that my parents would tell me I was going to be okay, to keep the faith, and to not give up and stay strong. This was so comforting and I believe it was one of those love touches from God.

One Friday afternoon, I arrived home and found myself sobbing. But I wasn't alone. God heard me and sent a tiny miracle my way. The phone rang. It was my CPA who had helped my ex-husband and me for over twenty years. He only needed to have some papers signed, but the miracle was that I had someone on the other end of the phone to talk with.

God sent an angel at that particular moment to help me endure the evening. He was a business friend who spent thirty minutes on the phone talking about nothing. Now *that* was a miracle!

It's important to accept those little angel visits and to know that the Lord hears your cries and wants to help you with His infinite power, peace, and comfort. When I finished the phone call, which I am sure meant nothing to my CPA, I thanked God. Please remember to answer those phone calls, emails, or texts as that is one way for God to lift up your mood and shower you with His love and grace.

Pray continually; give thanks in all circumstances, for this is God's will for you in Christ Jesus. 1 Thessalonians 5:17-18

As it says in 1 Thessalonians, God commands us to be thankful in *all* circumstances. Why? Because it's good for our hearts. When we thank Him in whatever we are facing, we are focused on His all-loving, all-powerful presence and not on our difficulties.

Thanking God for our countless blessings allows Him to bless us even more with peace, comfort, hope, joy, and most of all, His presence. God wants to know that we appreciate all He is doing. He, too, wants to be acknowledged and appreciated. We must thank Him for sending a person, a phone call, a card, or letter to break the loneliness.

I found that as I walked through my healing process, I was beginning to experience an amazing life with my Lord. I realized that in trusting Jesus in all things (although especially difficult at the beginning), my life became a role model and voice for others.

Without realizing it, my friends were watching and weighing my behavior. My sons were noticing my reactions and responses to the upcoming divorce. How my sons would treat their father, who they had lost all faith in and wanted nothing to do with, had a great deal to do with how I treated him. I needed to be forgiving, understanding, and caring because that is what God was expecting from me.

I heard early on from the Lord that I needed to forgive him and not take revenge, no matter how strong the desire. I remember how my ex-husband feared that I would tell his mistress's husband of their affair and potentially upend her financial security and that of her then husband.

I must admit, the temptation to alert the other spouse was strong as I didn't want him to be blindsided, as well, but I could hear God speaking to me to leave it to someone else.

Unfortunately, I didn't start out with those honorable characteristics or strong ethics, but as my walk with Jesus grew, I realized that taking the high road was the only way to go. I still became angry, frustrated, and hurt, and, yes, jealous. I had to ask for forgiveness many times and keep encouraging my sons to mend and continue in the relationships with their father.

As we walk through those cloudy, stormy, and, at times, very dark days of our lives, it is imperative to walk with Jesus. He is truly our light and the way. I look back on my situation and realize I would not be the person I am today, would not have the blessings I have today, nor would my life be filled with love, grace, and family had I taken up the evil of revenge and anger.

So, here's my question to you: Are you walking with Jesus? Are you keeping the devil at your back so you don't say or do things you may regret?

Will you write in your journal a promise to be honorable and gracious no matter how strong the anger becomes?

____

____

____

____

____

It certainly isn't easy in the beginning, but the outcome will bless you beyond your dreams.

The Calling to Write

I journaled through those trying years of which six years were the worst. I read scripture that lifted me up, inspired me to love and trust Jesus, and reminded me that all would be well, and this is key: *in God's perfect timing*.

Be strong and courageous...the Lord your God will be with you wherever you go. Joshua 1:9

Several months into my journaling (June 2003, to be exact), the word "book" flashed in my head. I asked, "Lord, did You send this thought?"

I heard, "*Write a book for prayers, for heartbreaks, for strength, for comfort, for courage, for all occasions. A Christian walk-through adversity.*"

This made sense, so I began to understand what God had planned for me.

Several years passed. I continued to journal, but never forgot the message that the Lord sent to me. I shared my thoughts with friends and one girlfriend suggested I write a blog. I didn't really know what a blog was, but just as quickly, it made sense. I could write a blog about my life experiences with the Lord.

What would it be about, specifically? Building a personal relationship with Jesus and loving and trusting God while rejoicing in the Holy Spirit.

First Blog: Old Dreams, New Opportunities, Finding Peace

Our everyday lives are blessings; however, everyone has times when life feels like one overwhelming challenge or maybe a stream of struggles and difficulties to maneuver through. When in the midst of the storm, it is nearly impossible to see clearly, but walking in trust and faith keeps us close to God.

The joy that comes from persevering is the gift of looking back on those situations and seeing clearly that God was guiding us through them all. We can see how God gave us small miracles, like friends or new opportunities that fulfilled long-forgotten dreams or goals.

It is through these struggling and challenging times that we find an inner strength, a new confidence, and brighter outlook that tell us that we are ready for the opportunities God has for us.

Those who respect the Lord ... He will point them to the best way ... My eyes are always looking for the Lord for Help. He will keep me from any traps. Psalms 25:12, 15

As we look to the Lord, let us continue to hold tight to Jesus as we praise His name.

God did have a plan for me. I wasn't sure at the time, but I now believe He was guiding me to help others. After all, God gave me the gift of gab. Ask anyone who knows me! My stories are full of details and rarely short!

So, as you walk through your challenges, trials, or disappointments, remember to look forward and find God's rainbow. Some of those rainbows are invisible, but trust in Him and know they are there, waiting for you. His promise is to always be there for you. His plan for you will always be far better than what you could ever think or imagine.

Chapter 5

The Stupid Stage

I need to keep moving forward. Help me focus on You, Jesus. Be with me as I venture forward. Please keep me from denial and fantasy.

- Journal Entry (March 2004)

As I write, please note that I still experience time in the "wilderness." I feel like the Israelites trying to get to the promised land. In the beginning of my journey with divorce, I am quite sure I complained and whined as much as they did, and my only hope was that it would not take forty years to reach my destination.

Although, my recovery would have been easier and faster with anxiety medication, my stubbornness would not give in to it. I wanted to feel strong and independent. I didn't want any help from anyone. however, I was having trust issues and felt that trusting in the Lord alone was the only way to get through my ordeal.

Please! Love yourself and get all of the help and support that you require as you walk in your own wilderness. There is nothing wrong with medication or other forms of help if they help you!

I now pray for God's wisdom, grace, and peace as I seek to bring my sisters and brothers of divorce solace and support from their aching hearts and disappointments. Being a sister in divorce is not the club I would have preferred, but now that I am here, I know that making the trek to health, healing, and emotional well-being is done through God and Jesus Christ—and sometimes doctors. Amen.

The name of the Lord is a strong defense, the godly run to him and are safe. The human spirit can endure a sick body, but who can hear a crushed spirit? Proverbs 18:10-11,14

Jesus understands pain, fear, and loneliness. I have often wondered if Jesus felt alone as a young man. Just think about the knowledge He had that no one else knew.

As a young boy speaking in synagogues, did people think Him odd? Did He keep to Himself? Regardless, Jesus made many walks by Himself. Even many of His family and friends didn't believe in Him. How lonely and disappointed He must have felt.

Yet Jesus trusted God. He knew He had a job to do and resolved to accomplish it. You have a job to do, too. Survive your divorce and become the person God planned for you to be from the beginning of time.

God does not expect us to stay the same. He wants growth, especially spiritual growth. Jesus wants a deep, personal relationship with us. He wants us waking up each morning and saying, "Thank you, dear Lord, for this beautiful day. What will we do together today?"

I did thank Jesus daily; however, I would become angry with my constant prayers of hope when I wasn't getting immediate satisfaction. We live in a world of immediate gratification, and I was acting like a young child demanding that our Father ease my pain and discomfort *now*!

Our instantaneous world began years ago when credit cards came along. We no longer had to wait for payday or save our money to buy the things or put them on layaway. We could see it, want it, and buy it right then!

We then progressed to computers, emails, text messages, and don't forget the cell phone that stays connected 24/7. Now, we get everything instantly, even at two in the morning!

I can't count how many times I have turned my car around because, "Oh, my goodness, I forgot my cell phone!" Talk about Panicville! And when I discuss this subject with my university students, they laugh and say the same thing. Okay, I digress.

I was having such a pity party! Please remember to love yourself, but not so much that you lose a healthy sense of reality.

How distressed God must get with our impatience and petulance. While I was praying and asking for help, I was thinking of the past. Just like the Israelites, I wanted my past, as broken as it was. I wanted to still be married to my ex-husband. Never mind that he had repeatedly lied, cheated, and betrayed me. Despite all of that, I was struggling to look at and want what God wanted for me.

God knew I deserved someone in my life who was honest, God-fearing, and honorable. If my ex-husband could not be that man, then God had a much better plan for me, which may or may not have included a new husband. It's okay if we live our lives with only family and friends and not a husband. Apostle Paul stated that to be single was better than to be married because it left more time for ministry (1 Cor. 7:8, 32) and there is definitely more to a woman's identity than being married.

We are first and foremost God's daughters and with God's blessings, a sibling, mom, cousin, auntie, friend, and maybe co-worker.

Many times, even up to five years after our separation and divorce (which took four of those years), my family and friends would tell me I couldn't go forward if I continued clinging to the past. In my head, I knew that, but my heart wasn't ready to accept it. So, I continued frittering away time in the wilderness.

When I say that my heart wasn't willing to accept my new reality, that didn't mean I wasn't trying to. But having been so blindsided, and then dealing with the effects PTSD, my heart was having trouble keeping pace with my brain. I would have to do a reset.

My brain would set the mood for the moment, hour, or day, then my PTSD would rise up and all I wanted was my old life back. I would rant and rave with anger and frustration, then fifteen or twenty minutes later, my brain would click in again and I would pray for God to help as I realized, once again, that PTSD was interfering with my healing.

If you, too, have PTSD, I pray that you are seeing a doctor, a counselor, or both. It is essential that you care for yourself so you can take care of others. Now, as I reflect on my journey, I remember having to repeat to myself to keep my focus on the future. This is known as "self-talk" and it is too often underestimated. It's also why it's so important to stay in the Word. It holds God's truths that we need to remember and practice, so that when irrational or negative thoughts and feelings begin to overtake our minds, we can beat them back with His wisdom and strength.

Take a moment and pray this prayer: Remind me, Lord, that there is a reason I have two eyes in the front of my head and not the back, to always look forward as I enjoy the day and embrace the future.

I found this great reminder from Wayne Dyer that is good advice for everyone since looking back is never a good idea, "Change the way you look at things and the things you look at change." "Fearless Motivation"

If you're only going to wish for things, you can't have or focus on painful experiences. Also, make sure that whatever advice you're taking in lines up with the Bible since it's the only source of genuine truth. When you find a verse or quote that helps you maintain helpful thoughts, put it somewhere you frequently visit so you'll be sure to see it often.

I printed and posted Dyer's quote in my bathroom, office, and kitchen. When I needed an uplifting thought, I would think about the quote. It was another reminder to look toward the future and trust God for His perfect will, even if it was still going to be hard at times.

It is all about perspective. If our outlook and mindset remain negative, then our thoughts and emotions will be, too. Thankfully, God's grace and mercies don't depend on our attitude, but we're in a much better place to receive them and give Him His due when our minds and hearts are fixed on Him and His perfect love.

So, I realized that I needed to think beyond the hurt, disappointment, and anger and look toward a brighter, more joyful future. It was waiting for me and it's waiting for you, too.

Have you found quotes, scriptures, or readings that empower you? Have your ideas and thoughts become positive strategies for a successful end to the divorce? If so, print them out, repeat them, and keep them handy.

You need to keep moving forward toward God's perfect plan for you.

What a sweet day it will be when you reach a place when life's challenges don't feel so much like trials as opportunities to see and demonstrate God's goodness and glory. It is then that you will also start seeing His miracles, blessings, and grace that have been there all along.

Depend on the Lord in whatever you do, and your plans will succeed. Proverbs 16:3

Chapter 6

The Handshake

You are my stronghold, my protection, dear God. I continue to do well, get stronger, and be a better person. To have patience, do the right thing, and to follow You, Lord. - Journal Entry (June 2003)

Now, more than a decade later, I look back on my walk through the divorce, heartache, and betrayal and find the joy of each day. My trust in God was a gift and I developed a close, personal relationship with Jesus that never leaves me. I know there is nothing I cannot accomplish with the Lord at my side.

My prayer for you and your walk through the challenges and tough times is that you, too, will find the sweet part of your day. May you feel the love of God and know that Jesus walked with you to your own promised land.

After trying to find my own partner in life through online dating (which was a huge mistake for me), I once again asked God for forgiveness and told Him that the only way I would have a relationship with a man was if He brought him to me.

Online dating was not for me because the men I found through it had very different ideas of what dating meant. For example, I received a phone call one night from a man wanting to come over at 9:30! I was getting ready for bed and had to work the next day.

Of course, I declined his request, but he persisted, saying that he was on his way. Again, I gave my regrets and told him that I wasn't available at such a late hour. Luckily, I lived in a gated community so that when he arrived, I was safe from his unwelcome imposition. Frankly, I was shocked and disgusted at his inappropriate and bold behavior, especially given my polite but firm protests. It goes without saying that we never spoke again.

Ladies, be aware that your ideas and wants, like a coffee date or a friendly dinner, will likely look quite different to the men you might find out there. Be strong and resolute in your values and morals. Keep the secular world at your back and proceed only with someone who wants to walk with the Lord, as well, and not just because you do.

Be very careful, then, how you live- not as unwise but as wise., making the most of every opportunity, because the days are evil. Therefore, do not be foolish but understand what the Lord's will is. Ephesians 5:15-17

Of course, living alone was not all bad. I slowly built a routine that worked for me and you will, too. It just takes time to find your rhythm and comfort with the change. I found my work satisfying and it kept me busy. I worked as a school counselor, an adjunct at two of our community colleges, and then our Christian university, where I continue to teach. I learned to reach out to others, go to movies, lunches, or school plays or sports.

Every summer, my brother, Tom and sister-in-law, Bev and I would do a road trip to our home state of South Dakota. At times, our youngest brother, Cary and his wife, Joan, would join us. What fun memories and such laughter!

We even made several stops in Colorado to watch our middle brother, Dave, play professional baseball for the Rockies. If his team was at home, it was a side trip we looked forward to. Our pride for him was button busting and full of cheering, not to mention that stadium dog and soda. This brings a smile to my face just thinking about all those great times.

These kinds of adventures can still happen if you give yourself permission to embrace your new normal. Never stop living; just make necessary adjustments.

Although it took me time, I finally reached a point where I could think seriously about dating again. I was looking for an honorable guy who loved the Lord and who enjoyed similar activities.

One day at church, I was chatting with a girlfriend and said, "Nancy, if you know of a nice Christian guy, please introduce us."

At the time, she didn't know of any, but a year later, she asked me to a super bowl party to meet this nice guy. I had a cold and was not in the mood, but I still went, wanting to be a good sport and see what the Lord might have in mind.

For whatever reason, this nice guy I was supposed to meet never ventured my way. He stayed glued to the television and spoke to only a couple of people, but when he was about to leave, he came over to say goodbye and stated, "Nice to meet you." He took hold of my hand with both of his and, in that instant, the love I felt from holding Jesus's hand years before coursed through my body for an instant.

I was shocked, to say the least, and couldn't understand what had just happened. Days later, I told Nancy about the handshake, not the part of holding the hand of Jesus, only that I had had a strange sensation when he took my hand.

Although he was a widower of a year and not ready to date, she still wanted us to meet, just in case he was open to making the dating leap again. My thought was on the handshake and felt strongly that God had a plan for me and him sometime in the future.

His name is Michael, and over the next couple of years, we met several times before venturing out on our first official date. Nancy and Richard invited us to a couples' dinner, which brought us together, but unbeknownst to me, he was shy and unsure of how to ask me out. To me, he seemed disinterested. Despite my previous feelings and hopes, I dismissed any ideas of us getting together, but then I would think about the handshake. Oh, my goodness, that amazing handshake! God's miracles come in many ways.

This is when you allow God to open doors or clear the path for your new opportunities and future. I didn't push my way into Michael's life, but I let God open the door.

Now, at this time, I experienced a downsizing in my employment due to the university's shrinking budget. Remember, God is always clearing the road that He has for you. Since I had spare time, I joined a singing and dancing performing group called New Wrinkles. It was for people fifty-five years and older who still wanted to be active. At the same time, Michael had decided to get out and meet more people with the same New Wrinkles group. God's best laid plans.

What an amazing and talented group of people! As we began rehearsals, which went for four months before our eighteen performances commenced, Michael and I, once again, got to see each other and get a bit more acquainted. He asked Nancy for my name. After several weeks of practice, he finally ventured a "hello" during one of our breaks.

He walked over to where I was sitting with several friends and Nancy's husband, Richard. The first question Michael asked after sitting down was, "How old are you?" Can you believe that?! Well, like any gal in that position, I was about to say fifty-five, as I generally do not go around stating my age, when Richard jumped in and followed up with, "Didn't you graduate from high school in 1965?"

"Yes," I replied. After all, I needed to admit my age, right? What I did not know was that Michael's father had remarried a woman twenty years his junior and it turned out bad. I look young for my age (God's blessing), but as it turns out, we were the same age. After that, he finally asked me out for our first date. The rest is history, as they say. Almost. Remember, it took me a long time to want to seriously date and my trust issues were huge and behind a tall thick brick wall.

As we began dating, thirteen years since my divorce, Michael could tell that I was struggling to trust his words and to let down my guard. God had brought me an amazing man who loved the Lord, was honest, had a strong moral compass, a tremendous amount of integrity, and an unwavering commitment to his vows. These were all the qualities I wanted in a husband.

Yet, I was still unwilling to step out from behind my fears and mistrust. How do I know this? I had built a large wall around my heart. You know the kind: ten feet high and ten feet thick with a sign yelling, "Do not trespass!"

Now, I was asking myself, "Do I take the leap of faith? How will I know if this is right?"

By trusting God.

Maybe you, too, have questioned God. It's okay to question Him; just be sure to pray and allow Him to set your future in motion.

Michael told me much later that he would rack his brain trying to figure out how he could infiltrate my inner wall so I could see that he was worthy of my trust.

On one of our Sunday afternoon drives, he told me that he wanted to show me something at the Veterans Memorial. We walked around the building and looked around a bit before he guided me toward a particular area. There, on a shelf behind glass, was Michael's name and commendation. He had been awarded the Distinguished Flying Cross for his amazing leadership, duty, and over 270 successful missions through dangerous conditions in Vietnam.

Before me was this amazing man. A quiet, humble, Christian man who hoped that showing me a tangible symbol of his dedication and valor would finally convince me that he was safe to trust and worth loving. Michael wasn't bragging or showing off—quite the contrary. He was simply trying to prove to me that he was a loyal man of God who could be trusted with my heart.

With God's help, my wall began to thin and eventually disappear. And with God's help, I made it to my promised land with Michael. Would I have found the promised land without Michael? Of course, but I believe my life was given another chance at marriage with someone who would show me the richness of living with someone who truly valued their spouse.

Now, if you are expecting me to write, "and they lived happily ever after," that is only in fairytales. Let's remember that I had lived alone for over thirteen years and that Michael had made many of the decisions in his life with his first wife. So, we were joining two strong personalities.

Michael has a powerful career as a CPA and forensic analyst. He is the specialist who goes to the trials with attorneys and testifies whether they had stated the truth or not. He could testify for one hour or for several. He has to be reliable and honest or risk losing all credibility.

Now, let's add that we both have strong, ingrained points of view and habits. I was the warm and fuzzy personality who wanted everyone to be happy and would happily help someone to achieve their goals with words of encouragement and support. I believed that every endeavor could follow a variety of paths.

Michael is a "give me the facts and only the facts" kind of guy. Results must always end with the correct answer and there was only one way to achieve it. I would joke that his patience was the length of a nanosecond.

Any relationship, not just those of older adults who have already been married, involves adjustments, compromises, and lots of discussions. So as Michael and I began our lives together, we knew through a few miscommunications that we would need to adapt some of our habits.

I enjoy semi-lengthy telephone conversations and must remember that Michael wants only the facts. I accommodate his need for shorter conversations by leaving out less important details. On the other hand, Michael is sensitive to my needs and offers me the quality time I like and prays out loud with me every night.

We are both strong Christians with a mutual love for God and Jesus Christ; however, we didn't attend the same church when we met. To remedy this, we decided to attend both churches at first to find the best fit for us as a couple.

I am forever grateful for his loving willingness to join my church. We now both actively serve and attend adult Sunday school and church services. I thank God daily for bringing such a godly man into my life. His love and respect are over the top as is his decision to leave his church friends and family of several years and begin a new church life with me.

That's what love and respect look like.

Have you thought about ways you can show love and respect? Feel free to jot them down in your journal, if you are using one. If not, find quotes that are pertinent, cut them out, and display them for great reminders of God's grace to us.

____

____

____

____

____

Continue to pray so you understand the true meaning of love and respect as you build or refresh your relationship with Jesus and move forward with a new relationship in your life. Pick up your Bible, find faith-based books to read, and immerse yourself in wonderful Christian music and movies.

Those who know your name trust in you, for you, Lord have never forsaken those who seek you. Psalm 9:10

We also used our humor, age, and experiences as well as our love for each other and God. One funny thing we still laugh about was the time the batteries for the TV remote control went out. He became frustrated, threw the remote down, and stormed out of the house.

When he returned with new batteries, I put my hands on his face and said, "Did my little warrior get those new batteries?" Then I smiled and he smiled, and we broke out laughing. Like I said, use humor to get through frustrating situations, not anger or harsh words. We want to lift our loved ones up, not put them down.

I remember our first trip after being married a year. We took a seven-day cruise and had a wonderful time. When we arrived at the Los Angeles terminal for our departure, the parking lot was full as there were two cruise ships leaving about the same time.

Our only alternative was to park about twenty minutes from the entrance of the boarding area and walk to the terminal pulling our luggage along a rough, hole-ridden, and bumpy pavement. What a way to start our vacation! Why we didn't drop off our luggage at the terminal, I have no idea.

As the experience of togetherness continued, let's remember that I was okay with all of the inconveniences. After all, we were still newly married and the honeymoon stage was alive and well! It was the return trip to the car after our trip was done that caused concern.

We brought our luggage out of the cruise terminal and Michael suggested I stay behind while he retrieved the car. *Yay*! I thought. *I don't have to lug our belongings to the car! Such a sweet and caring husband.*

Unbeknownst to me, it was about to rain. I don't mean a little sprinkle or a five-minute passing shower; we had a downpour that lasted forty minutes. All the while, I was standing in this deluge of water, waiting for that sweet husband of mine.

He drove up to the curb and jumped out yelling, "Hurry up! I am getting wet!"

Really?! I had been standing in the downpour for over thirty minutes with only a fleece jacket over my head and he was using language that was hard to hear just because his shirt was getting wet. Pray for me, right? Do the self-talk. Do not yell. Smile!

After we got in the car, I took off my wet clothes and opened a suitcase for a dry top and pants. Nothing more was said about me being soaked and his shirt being a tiny bit wet. The laugh came when we drove into the driveway, took out our luggage, and I threw the fleece jacket onto the driveway since it was wet.

We had driven four and half hours home, and as the jacket lay on the driveway, the water began to run down our driveway to the curb. It was completely saturated. Michael looked at it and was speechless. He stated, "I had no idea you were that wet."

I tell this story because we have had so many belly laughs over this. He was upset because his shirt was getting wet while I was a drowned puppy. Because he had to walk so far to the car, the deluge didn't reach him until he arrived at our car, safe and dry. He truly had no idea I was so wet!

We now joke about who is going to get the car. I take the keys and run for it or make sure I have an umbrella!

Our lives are not perfect, but the memories are full of joy and God's love. It truly doesn't get any better than that.

As you travel your path, join the Lord on your pilgrimage to your promised land and know that if you entrust, truly entrust, all areas of your life to Jesus, the end results will be joyful and stunning, though not always easy. Even so, God's light will fill your heart and you will know that you, too, have reached the promised land.

The word of the Lord is right and true He is faithful in all He does. Psalm 33:4

Thank you, Lord, for each day, for all of the challenges, trials, and tears. You have showered me with unfathomable joy, mercy, and grace. I pray that I always follow Your path and lead the life you have chiseled out for me. I thank You for the mustard seed of faith that has grown beyond my wildest dreams.

As you travel to your promised land through your challenges and tribulations, remember to trust God and hang tightly to Jesus. We are blessed beyond any gift we could imagine, and He will never leave us nor fail us; therefore, my house will choose the Lord.

But as for me and my household, we will serve the Lord. Joshua 24:15

Conclusion

Trust in the Lord with all your heart and lean not on your own understanding, in all your ways submit to hm and he will make your paths straight.

Proverbs 3:5-6

I believe I have now come full circle with my saga of betrayal, denial, and sadness as I learned to trust God and build my personal life with Jesus Christ. The joys, the friendships, and the love were a bounty of blessings I could not have imagined.

I thank God daily for this life of prayer, the mustard seed of faith that has grown as tall and strong as a redwood tree in California, and the opportunity to share my faith with family and friends, and my work with my students in a Christian university. My cup overflows as I am known as a prayer warrior, a title that showers me with an attitude of gratitude. What could be better than that?

If you are continuing with your journal, take the time to pen your thoughts, say a prayer of thanksgiving, and trust God in all ways. Remember, He is always waiting to enter your life. Open the door and receive all that God has in store for you.

Thank you for taking this walk with me.

Blessings,

Cynthia

Printed in the USA
CPSIA information can be obtained
at www.ICGtesting.com
LVHW011539240824
789107LV00007B/196

9 798868 500992